Contents

A diet this is certainly plant-based prioritizing plant foods—specifically minimally processed fruits, veggies, whole grains, beans, legumes, nuts, and seeds, says Joseph. What that like that is looks vary from person to person, however.

For instance, if you follow a Mediterranean diet, you can easily be mostly plant-based, prioritizing items legumes that is like nuts, healthy fats, fruits and veg, and avoiding fish. If you're keto, it may possibly be a harder that is small follow since the keto diet nixes more carb-rich foods like wholegrains, starchy vegetables, and fruit, but it can be done. (Plant-based keto is a thing!)

And plant-based doesn't necessarily plant-exclusive that is mean. Though veganism is a type of plant-based diet, you don't have to cut out all animal products forever to consider yourself a eater this is certainly plant-based. (Plus, not all vegan foods tend to be naturally plant-based; egg-free brownies might be vegan, but they're not truly plant-based if they're packed with processed ingredients.)

"I consider myself plant-based because most of the foods I eat are plants," says Joseph. "That said, I also eat yogurt, cheese, eggs, and fish when I feel like it, and that's okay!"

A diet that is plant-based any diet that focuses around foods derived from plant resources. This can include fruit, vegetables, grains, pulses, legumes, nuts and meat substitutes such as soy products.

People often have different interpretations of exactly what 'plant-based' eating looks like. Some people still include small amounts of animal products such as meat and fish, while focusing mainly on vegetarian foods – this is referred to as a semi-vegetarian or diet that is flexitarian. Plans that cut out meat but seafood that is still include referred to as pescatarian diets. Men and women who don't meat that is eat fish but still include milk and eggs are referred to as vegetarian, while those who cut out any animal derived products, including dairy, eggs, honey and gelatin are referred to as vegan.

People following diets that is plant-based consuming a multitude of fruits, veggies and pulses are most likely to think it is more straightforward to meet their five-a-day target. Due to this, they tend to be also to that is likely good intakes of fibre and the vitamins and minerals that are present in fruit and vegetables, including folate, vitamin C and potassium, all of which are important for good wellness.

But, it is worth noting that 'plant-based' does not automatically imply 'healthy', particularly when it comes to processed and packaged foods. Technically, items such as refined sugar, white flour and certain vegetable fats can all be labelled 'plant-based' that they should make up the volume of a healthy diet as they are vegetarian, but this does not mean.

A plant-based diet is any diet that focuses plants first that is on. This includes nutrient-dense fresh fruits, veggies, nuts, seeds, whole grains and legumes. With that said, plant-based does not have to mean plant-exclusive. Moderate amounts of meat, chicken, fish, seafood, eggs and dairy could all be included. Simply put, when following a plant-based diet you're choosing to more plants that is eat.

Plant-based eating may summon a particular kind of imagery: rustic grains and kale that is bountiful golden turmeric tinctures, earthenware bowls overflowing with farmers market roughage.

But beyond the romance, what does this kind of eating entail that is actually? A vegan diet for some, it mimics.

Others carry on to work products that is animal like honey or cheese, into the arsenal. While the term has surged in popularity in recent years, it lacks a definition this is certainly clear-cut.

All of the chefs I spoke with seem to agree that "plant-based" connotes more of the holistic lifestyle, rather than an set that is ironclad dos and don'ts.

Selection of Plant-Based Diets

A diet that is plant-based of mainly whole, plantbased foods like whole grains, legumes (beans, peas, lentils), veggies, fruits, seeds, and nuts. There are many different sorts of plant-based diets and they are categorized based on the meat that is extent included. Some regarding the more popular ones include semi-vegetarian or flexitarian, pescatarians, lacto-ovo vegetarian, and vegans. Here is a summary of vegetarian diets:

Semi-vegetarian or flexitarian is someone who is primarily a vegetarian but will also consume small amounts of meat, poultry, fish, and seafood. They also might dairy that is include and eggs. This type of eating is more compared that is flexible something like a vegan diet and is a good starting place for individuals looking to incorporate more plant-based meals. Pescatarians are individuals who are primarily vegetarian, but they consume that is also will and fish.

Lacto-ovo vegetarian diet is a diet that is plant-based also includes eggs and dairy products. The diet excludes meat, fish, poultry, and any products that contain these foods.

Vegan diets exclude meat, eggs, and products that is dairy. Vegans additionally exclude all ingredients that is animal-derived. An note this is certainly important vegans is the importance of vitamin B-12. Vitamin B-12 is located only in animal foods, some fortified cereals, or some nutritional yeast, so vegans need certainly to take vitamin B-12 as a supplement to ensure intake that is adequate.

There many that is are plant-based diets that individuals may choose to follow. An fact this is certainly important any of these vegetarian eating plans or diets is that they can work for everyone and individuals have the choice of what they want to include or exclude.

What Can You Eat on a Plant-Based Diet

When picturing what a meal that is plant-based like, fruits and vegetables probably come to mind. And they're an essential part of only about any diet this is certainly healthy. But not that is you're to these foods. There are a number this is certainly wide plant foods to enjoy. The major types of food typically eaten on a diet include that is plant-based

- Fruits — Ex: Apples, fruits, kiwis, mangoes, avocado, bananas, jackfruit, etc.

- veggies — Ex: Onions, broccoli, beets, potatoes, mushrooms, carrots, etc.

- Whole grains — Ex: Quinoa, millet, buckwheat, wheat, rice, corn, etc.

•	Beans & legumes — Ex: Black beans, chickpeas, lentils, edamame, peas, etc.

•	Nuts & seeds — Ex: Almonds, cashews, chia seeds, flaxseeds, walnuts, etc.

•	Herbs & herbs — Ex: Turmeric, ginger, cinnamon, oregano, garlic, cayenne, etc.

•	Fermented foods — Ex: Kimchi, sauerkraut, miso, natto, etc.

Eating across all these food groups will help you get an abundance of micronutrients from your food. Also, when choosing from each category, think "eat the rainbow." Colorful plant foods are full of phytochemicals (a fancy word that just means "chemicals from plants) and antioxidants that are good for keeping different parts of your body healthier.

Exactly how to start a plant based diet for beginners

Are you ready to get started? Unveiling, our most comprehensive list yet: how to start a plant based diet for beginners! Here's to that are what:

Review the recipes, detailed by type. A plant based list this is certainly foods overwhelming. Here we've organized our recipes by type. Plant based revolves which are eating main types of recipes based on function, from soups to sandwiches to tacos to breakfasts to snacks.

Keep in mind plant based necessary protein. Most of the recipes below are loaded with plant based protein. Assessment the above that is list and if necessary serve with a side that includes it. A salad this is certainly side nuts and seeds or even a handful of almonds works.

Pick one and start! You don't have to know everything before you get started if you're looking to take up a plant based diet. Just pick one recipe and make it! It, great if you like! Save that for future years. Or even, move on and keep trying things until you develop your tastes.

Plant-Based Diet vs Vegan Diet Plan

We all by now have heard of family or friends that have gone "vegan" or have adopted a "plant-based diet." Others may even know people on a "whole-food, plant-based diet." Some of this terminology is relatively new; some of it features a history that is longer. Further confusing things is these that is how are quickly evolving and often mean different things to different men and women. But what do terms that are these to most of us today? Let's take a much deeper dive.

What Is the Difference Between a Vegan Diet and a Plant-Based Diet

An eating plan this is certainly plant-based consists of plants; most people use the term to refer to a 100 percent plant diet, but some folks include small amounts of animal products. A diet that is vegan eliminates all animal items.

11

The vast majority of food comes from plants with a plant-based diet. The term originated in the health science community, where it was more proper than "vegetarian" or "vegan." First, the term is divorced from any connotation this is certainly ethical and second, it doesn't mean "never eating meat" or "never eating animal products." Consumption of very tiny amounts of animal foods can be inconsequential whenever speaking of this health benefits of a diet, a significant nuance for science that is not captured by the term "vegan" or "vegetarian."

Is a diet this is certainly plant-based

Vegetables, fruits, whole grains, legumes like dried beans and lentils, and nuts each offer a unique package of nutrients, plant compounds and dietary fiber that can protect heart health. For example, dried beans and lentils offer viscous forms of dietary fiber that can help lower blood cholesterol and fiber that is fermentable may help reduce inflammation that may lead to heart infection.

Variety is the key, since other meals that are plant nutrients and natural plant compounds like polyphenols that can help lower hypertension.

An analysis of observational studies involving more than four people that are million the world links eating habits that most closely found qualities of the traditional Mediterranean diet with less heart disease incidence and deaths. Scores reflect plant-focused diet programs, with points added for abundant plant meals and subtracted for meat or dairy products more than once a day. Many studies also link vegetarian diets with a lower risk of heart disease. Yet various versions of the DASH diet, which concentrates on an abundance of plant foods, but does integrate lean meat and two to three servings daily of low-fat dairy products, have reduced LDL ("bad") cholesterol and bloodstream pressure in randomized trials that is managed.

Does a diet help prevent disease that is plant-based

A diet this is certainly plant-based a vital foundation of recommendations to reduce cancer risk. Different forms of dietary fiber can each play a job in protection against colon disease, and perhaps other cancers, too. And whole grains may offer security beyond the they provide that is fiber. Laboratory studies show lots of mechanisms through which and that is nutrients found in plant foods can steer cells away from developing into cancer, from changes in expression of tumor suppressor and other genes, to influences on cell signaling pathways, irritation, and self-destruction of abnormal cells.

As research methods have advanced, human population studies are less consistent in help for individual antioxidant nutrients or specific plant meals for cancer prevention. But rather than concluding that these nutrients and compounds don't matter after all, the picture that is big of suggests that it's how they work together that matters. And people may differ importance this is certainly in the specific choices within a plant-based diet based on individual differences in genetics and microbiota.

Will I lose weight on a diet that is plant-based

A meal plan that is plant-based an exemplary approach to lose weight healthfully and keep it off. Because it includes substantial portions of foods like vegetables that are filling without being in that is high, it helps you cut calories without going hungry. Smartly chosen options of plant foods, alone or addition that is in modest portions of fish, poultry, eggs, dairy, and meat, can provide enough protein to minimize loss of muscle when you minimize calories for body weight loss. And although some plant-based diets tend to be very in that is low, plant-based diets can include reasonable portions of fats from nuts, avocados, and healthy oils that also help to keep hunger at bay.

Plant-based diets don't guarantee weight loss, however. Overdoing portions or snacking all day out of habit, or using food to deal with stress, can keep calories too high to weight reduction that is allow. And excess calories can add up quickly even from plant-based drinks, whether juice, carbonated drinks, syrup-laden coffees or alcohol.

Plant-based alone doesn't make it healthy.

Although highly foods that is processed chips, crackers, and cookies may technically be plant-based, these foods won't provide the health benefits you get from unprocessed and minimally processed alternatives. And enormous amounts of added sugars can that is and fat to eating more calories than you need.

When researchers scored eating habits in several large U.S. population studies as being more focused on plant meals or foods that is animal plant-based diets were linked with lower danger of heart disease. But when they scored healthful plant foods separately from less plant that is beneficial like sweets, sugar-sweetened drinks, and refined grains, men and women with healthy plant-based diets showed 25% lower risk of heart disease. But scores that is high unhealthy plant-based diets had 32% greater risk of heart disease and increased risk of type 2 diabetes as well.

You make an eating plan that is plant-based by what you choose to eat often, as well as what you limit.

Plant-based diets on a budget

Meat is one of the most items that are expensive your grocery cart. So whether you choose to have a few meatless meals each week or simply keep portion sizes of beef, poultry and fish little compared to various other foods on your plate, plant-focused eating is an excellent way to shave grocery prices.

Dried out beans, peas, and lentils, in contrast, are a bargain. Look beyond frozen convenience vegetarian meals and explore the aisles of canned and beans that is dried. If you've been making use of these only occasionally for beans that is baked tacos, have fun exploring the many dishes in which they fit deliciously.

Fruits and vegetables might seem too pricey to fit your budget, but that need not be so. Remember that as you boost portions of foods which are these it should be considered a swap to replace or reduce the amount of something different. For example, choose a piece of fruit instead of donuts, cookies or cream that is ice. When selecting fresh produce, look for what's in season. And overlook that is don't and canned options (without added salt or sugar), which can be just as healthy and may offer a much better buy.

Explore plain, unseasoned grains this is certainly whole season and serve with meals instead of high-priced flavored options. And choose simple cooked or ready-to-eat breakfast cereals like oatmeal or wheat that is shredded. Include nuts which are your own fruit, and maybe a sprinkle of cinnamon for flavor.

Cook home

Not only is cooking at home less costly than eating out, it also gives you more opportunity to experiment with different ways to create plant-focused meals. Some people find that adapting familiar dishes is the most way that is comfortable gradually change eating habits. For example, keep the same casserole or stew you love, and swap proportions to reduce meat and boost veggies beans that is and. For other folks, adapted versions always seem second best. Starting with that is fresh and different plant-focused dishes becomes an adventure.

You aren't alone exploring this turf this is certainly new explore the Resources below. Always check companies like the American Institute for Cancer Research (AICR) that recommend plant-based and that is diets delicious recipes to put their guidance into practice. Follow savvy registered dietitians on Facebook, Instagram or through their particular blogs for meals that are delicious and healthy. Websites of producers and businesses providing plant-based foods also offer menu ideas and taste-tested recipes (and often coupons) to help you step beyond a repertoire this is certainly limited.

Make Plant-based Flavorful

If you're afraid dishes which are plant-based be dull, think again! Some of the most cuisines that are flavorful the world are plant-based. Take inspiration from traditional Italian, Greek, Chinese and Indian dishes that make vegetables, grains and beans with that is tasty, onion, herbs, spices, and nuts.

Go at Your Own Pace

The is this is certainly goal get a hold of the right path to a lasting plant-based style of eating. So it's essential to discover what works for you, rather than making remarkable changes that don't comfortable that is feel.

Slowly move proportions of vegetables, grains, and meat in meals and add a few meatless meals this is certainly more.

Find a Diet this is certainly plant-Based that's for You

Many, many reports show that plant-based patterns that is eating a whole are healthier ways to eat than the eating style that's typical now in the U.S. (and many other parts for the globe). Whether referred to as a diet this is certainly western in research or S.A.D. (Standard American Diet) in more informal discussions, they're demonstrably behind plant-based diets for healthy eating. When looking at individual kinds of plant-based diets (vegetarian, DASH, etc.), studies conclude they are healthier than typical fare that is us. But that doesn't mean that the specific form of a plant-based diet is better than another approach to eating this is certainly plant-focused.

There's room in the"tent this is certainly plant-based for everyone, whether you prefer vegan or vegetarian eating, or want to include modest amounts of fish, chicken, and meat; whether you favor low-fat or relatively higher amounts of healthy types of fat.

Plant-Based Diet Grocery List

If you're a novice, right here's a plant-based diet food list with the key ingredients we recommend for starting a diet this is certainly plant-based. As you start experimenting with different plant-based dishes and understand which meals and components your body responds best to, you can expand your shopping list according that is plant-based.

•   Fruit and Vegetables: Banana, avocado, orange, apple, berries, onion, garlic, leafy greens, cabbage, carrots, beetroot, kumara, broccoli, cauliflower, zucchini, tomatoes, beetroot etc

- Wholegrains: Quinoa, buckwheat, oats, brown rice

Integrating into this is certainly wholegrains diet can be an inexpensive method to ensure you're finding a good intake of complex carbohydrates and dietary fibre to support healthy digestion and sustained energy levels. If you've never prepared with quinoa or buckwheat before, you can use these grains wherever you would use rice, typically and they make a perfect base for buddha bowls. Oats are always handy to have in the kitchen for making homemade granola, porridge or bircher muesli which makes a great snack that is mid-morning. My favourite way to cook grains is in the rice cooker you can leave the grains to cook while you do something else, or prep something else for dinner because this means. Pro tip - create a wholegrain flour by blending buckwheat that is entire a coffee grinder.

- Oils: Coconut oil and avocado oil (for frying, baking and treats that is raw, extra virgin olive oil (for dressings)

Coconut oil is arguably the most versatile oil to have on standby because you can use it in wholefood baking, raw sweets and frying this is certainly for. Both oil this is certainly avocado coconut oil tend to be resistant to oxidation at high heats which makes them perfect for frying. Reserve the extra virgin oil for making hummus and plant-based dressings (like those who work in the recipes overhead).

- Sauces: Coconut aminos or tamari (gluten-free soy sauce), preservative-free mustard

Tamari is soy that is gluten-free and coconut amios is a soy-free substitute which comes from coconut sap. These seasonings bring a flavour this is certainly brilliant dressings when blended with tahini and lemon juice or apple cider vinegar.

- Vinegars: Apple cider vinegar, balsamic vinegar

Apple cider vinegar is so you that is functional use it in dressings, cooking or as a digestive aid. You can even use it as a cleaning product which is household! Balsamic is brilliant to have on hand for dressings and is drizzled that is epic roast vegetables.

- Spices and seasonings: Turmeric, cumin, paprika, Himalayan sea salt, pepper, kelp, yeast flakes

Himalayan sodium that is sea key because it contains iodine (unlike regular sea salt), kelp is another great source of iodine which has a host of other health benefits too. Having spices like turmeric, cumin, coriander and paprika on hand is for that is perfect the flavour of roasted vegetables, making curry pastes or adding a kick to hummus or dressings. Yeast flakes have an original flavour this is certainly cheese-like are the most perfect substitute for parmesan cheese when sprinkled over a plant-based pizza or tomato-based dishes.

• Sweeteners: Raw honey, agave syrup, maple syrup, rice malt syrup, dates and/or various other good fresh fruit this is certainly dried

Raw honey has bonus antibacterial properties, but agave and maple syrup can be used as substitute sweeteners in pretty any dish that is much. Rice malt syrup is made totally from fermented brown rice and is a versatile option for those looking for a alternative that is fructose-free.

• Herbs: Coriander, parsley, basil

In the event that you don't grow these at home, do! Or you can select them up from your local farmers' market and experiment with the new varieties you can on get the hands. Herbs are handy dressings that is for salads, roast vegetables or even green smoothies!

Nuts, seeds and superfoods: Almonds, cashews, walnuts, Brazil nuts, pumpkin seeds, sunflower seeds, linseed, sesame seeds, chia seeds, cacao, goji berries, coconut, vanilla, dates, cinnamon, ginger - only to mention a few!

These tend to be basics in our pantry that is plant-based for everything from superfood smoothies, nut butters and bliss balls to pestos and salads.

- beverage: Chamomile, peppermint, green tea

Chamomile tea is the night this is certainly perfect and can help promote a better night's sleep. Peppermint is perfect if you're limiting your caffeine intake, and green tea is a go-to for any boost that is antioxidant.

- Legumes: Chickpeas, lentils, black colored beans

Chickpeas are necessary for buddha and hummus bowls, lentils for curries and soups, and beans for Mexican dishes. If you're excluding or minimising meat from your diet, legumes are the perfect replacement this is certainly plant-based a 1 cup serving of cooked black beans has around 15g of protein and 20% of the daily recommended intake of iron.

- Canned Foods: Coconut cream, chopped tomatoes

Coconut cream is convenient to have in your pantry for curries or your own yoghurt that is making. Chopped tomatoes are ideal for slow-cooking in winter and dishes this is certainly italian-style. Opt for BPA free cans wherever possible and keep your eye out for unwanted additives in the number that is ingredients.

- Fermented Foods: Coconut yoghurt, sauerkraut

Fermented foods like coconut yoghurt and sauerkraut (fermented vegetables) are basics in plant-based diet plans, as they can play an important role in improving the ratio of beneficial bacteria in your gut, which can in turn help support a immune system that is healthy.

•   Milks: Coconut milk, almond milk or cashew milk

Dairy-free milks are super easy to find in the or this is certainly supermarket make at home - see our how to make a smoothie like a boss guide for a homemade nut milk meal

•   Butters and spreads: Tahini and fan butter (ie. peanut butter, almond butter or cashew butter)

Tahini (ground sesame seeds) is an awesome supply of calcium for a plant-based diet and is super convenient for making hearty salad dressings or sauces that will take any plant-based meal to the amount that is next. Nut butters are also for that is brilliant, plant-based baking, raw treats and smoothie bowls!

• Utensils: Blender, food processor (or a device that doubles both that is as - and that's it!

Its not necessary invest that is to any fancy or expensive kitchen equipment to get begun having a plant-based diet - so there's no holding back now!

Plant-Based Diet Meal Plan

Developing a dinner this is certainly plant-based might be easier than you think. Here's our go-to diet that is plant-based plan which includes inspiration for breakfast, lunch, dinner, dessert and snack options. You can mix and match the different options to design a meal that is plant-based that works for you and the ingredients you have available in your kitchen area.

Plant-Based Diet Breakfast Ideas

Superfood smoothie: We may be biased, but there's better that is no to enhance your intake of plant-based nutrients than by having a different smoothie for breakfast each morning. By blending seasonal combinations of fresh fruit and vegetables with balancing superfood blends, you're going to be getting a wholefood source that is plant-based of fibre, protein, healthy fats, antioxidants, essential vitamins and minerals. Find out what you can expect breakfast this is certainly for Craft Smoothie.

Smoothie bowl: Try one of these super easy smoothie bowl recipes which are for that is ideal kids (and adults) engaged in healthy eating

Plant-Based Diet Snacks Ideas

- Chia pudding: Blend 1 cup of coconut water with 1 tablespoon of nut butter, 2 of this is certainly tbs seeds, a dash of your favourite sweetener and vanilla. Transfer the chia blend to a jar and fill up with a fruits which can be few your favourite superfoods.

- Bliss balls: For a bliss this is certainly basic recipe, all you need is dates, nuts, coconut and cacao and you're away! There are literally millions of different bliss ball recipes online, but do not be afraid to experiment with your own combinations and adjust the to that is fruit ratio to match. Pro tip - including oats is a cheap solution to bulk your bliss up balls and increase the fibre content.

- Kale chips: Wash and kale that is dry, drizzle with avocado oil or coconut oil and season with salt, kelp and nutritional yeast flakes. Bake for around 10 to 15 minutes at 180°C or the that is until tend to be brown.

Plant-Based Diet Lunch Ideas

•   Macro buddha bowl: discover how to make the buddha that is ultimate with this recipe above

•   Cabbage wrap with hummus, avocado and sauerkraut: Keep it simple with a gut-friendly, plant-powered and wrap that is protein-packed!

•   Seasonal salad with green protein dressing: Get crafty with new season salad ingredients so lunch never boring this is certainly gets. Scroll up for some recipe inspiration

Plant-Based Diet Plan Dinner Ideas

•   Zucchini noddles with lentil bolognese: Get your zoodle on with our tasty recipe above

- Plant-based pizza with gluten-free broccoli base: We're loving this broccoli crust pizza at that is recipe moment - it's awesome topped with hummus and pesto

- Black bean noodles with sun-dried tomato and basil pesto: See our plant-based dishes above to learn how to make this crafty take on a meal that is italian-style

Plant-Based Diet Dessert Ideas

- Turmeric latte: Here's our easy turmeric latte recipe that's ideal for a low sugar, nutrient-dense dessert

- Superfood chocolate: Curb your cravings by melting together 1 tablespoon of nut butter, 1 tablespoon of honey (or other sweeteners), 2 tablespoons of coconut oil and 1 tablespoon of cacao. Pour the melted mixture into a container lined with baking paper and with that is sprinkle favourite superfoods - coconut, goji berries and cacao nibs are a winning combo. Shop within the freezer set that is until do not forget to share!

Remember you don't have to make radical modifications to start out enjoying the benefits of a meal plan this is certainly plant-based. It's not about creating restrictions around what you can and can't eat, but more that is pretty adding wholefoods to your diet. And the benefits of eating up more plants will extend how that is beyond feel - you are going to start to notice the advantages from the outside too!

A try and we'll deliver everything you need to make 100% plant-based superfood smoothies at home if you want to experiment with a plant-based morning meal routine, give Craft Smoothie.

How can I get protein

Plant meals that tend to be based any foods that contain no pet products (meat, dairy, eggs, honey). Here's the most part that is important plant based eating: protein is key for staying satiated and full. Alex and I have already been doing this plant based thing this is certainly eating years. And we've learned the most part that is important of vegan and vegetarian recipes is to make sure they're packed with protein. If not, we'll be hungry an hour later on!

Luckily, there of that is lots for adding plant based protein to your meals to make them filling and healthful. Here's a plant based food list with the most notable foods that is protein-filled

•   Legumes: Try lentils (red, green, brown, French), separate peas, black-eyed peas, and beans (black, garbanzo / chickpeas, lima, navy, pinto, white, and kidney)

•   Grains: decide to try quinoa, barley, bulgur wheat, amaranth, millet, and and that is brown rice (see How to Cook Whole Grains)

•   Nuts and seeds: attempt almonds, cashews, peanuts, walnuts, pecans, hazelnuts, pistachios, pumpkin seeds, sesame seeds, sunflower seeds

•	Soy: Soy based products like tofu and tempeh are rich in plant based protein; follow 2 to 4 servings week this is certainly per.

•	Veggies: Some vegetables protein this is certainly have but in reduced amounts than the foods above. Some higher protein veggies are corn, broccoli, asparagus, Brussels sprouts, and artichokes. When eating that is you're of protein from plants, it's important to get a wide variety of protein sources.

What Do You Avoid on a Plant-Based Diet

Whenever choosing to eat a diet that is plant-based you'll want to concentrate mainly on fresh foods. Within a grocery store, that means primarily shopping the outer aisles. If at all possible, choose foods this is certainly natural much as possible to avoid exposure to GMOs and pesticides. However, the main foods you should avoid for a diet are that is plant-based

• Most or all animal products (Especially factory-farmed meat, eggs, & dairy products)

37

• Refined sugars (White sugar, cane sugar, high fructose corn syrup, chemical-based calorie-free sweeteners, etc.)

• definitely processed vegetable oils (Corn oil, cottonseed oil, sunflower oil, peanut oil, soybean oil, etc.)

• White flour (particularly bleached white flour which is full of chemicals and heavy metals — and virtually devoid nutrition that is of

• Junk food (Including most cookies, chips, crackers, snack taverns, sweetened drinks, packaged meals, etc.)

• GMOs (The primary genetically engineered crops are corn, soy, canola, sugar beets, cotton, and alfalfa plus a bit of apple, zucchini, and potato)

You'll also want to pay special attention to labels that is nutrition. By reading labels, you can avoid and this is certainly ultra-processed ingredients. Packaged foods should few have as ingredients as possible. As a rule that is general if you can't pronounce an ingredient, or don't know what it is, put the food back.

Many packed foods are of that is full claims like "all-natural" or "non-GMO." But most of these phrases are branding tactics meant to mislead consumers into thinking a product is healthy. This is called "greenwashing."

What Does Plant-Based Eating Look Like Each Day

So, how do these principles translate into real life on a basis that is day-to-day? For Wright, a normal day of eating might entail a warm porridge that is whole-grain good fresh fruit or a smoothie loaded with greens and healthy fats; grains and greens drizzled in a homemade sauce or dressing for lunch; and big salads loaded with grilled veggies, or perhaps a lentil-based pasta tossed with produce for dinner.

"It's very vegetable-forward. "The whole day, I'm trying to work fruits or vegetables into every meal, while grains and nuts are the supporting role."

39

The consensus seems to be that "plant-based" isn't only about not eating meat or trying to consume a predetermined amount of produce per day it's about celebrating plants, rather than relegating them to a side dish or augmenting them with meat substitutes, and doing so with integrity while the phrase, and just how it manifests, may look slightly different to everybody.

For some cooks, that means an opportunity to challenge yourself, working from a limited that is more of ingredients ultimately yields more creative results. "You have to work more difficult to create certain flavors and textures, but the rewards, I think, are far greater."

What's the difference between plant-based and diets that is vegan

A vegan diet is the most restrictive of plant-based diet plans. This is this is certainly diet around fruits, vegetables, whole grains, legumes, nuts and seeds. However, unlike other plant-based eating plans, the vegan diet contains zero ingredients that is animal-sourced. That means meat that is no poultry, seafood, dairy, eggs or honey.

People become vegan for many reasons – for the welfare of animals, the preservation of the planet, their personal that is own health more. Science suggests that vegan diets are more environmentally sustainable than food diets high in animal products and with that is associated health benefits. The good news is you don't have to banish your favorite foods to reap the health and environmental benefits of plant-based eating with that said, for those true meat lovers.

Why should you consider a diet that is plant-based

Whole food diets this is certainly plant-based filled up with produce, whole grains and plant proteins (i.e. peanuts, legumes), have been linked to a variety of benefits.

They provide essential nutrients and minerals, nourishing fiber and fats, as well as beneficial plant nutrients, which all contribute to wellbeing this is certainly overall. Several studies have shown that plant-based eating patterns help a number of health outcomes, including a healthy healthy and heart weight.

But, that's not all! Picking plants as the star of your meals and snacks isn't good that is only you – it is good for the planet too. A diet higher in flowers and lower in animal-based foods is associated with less of a impact on the environment than the typical American diet in fact, according to the 2015 Dietary Guidelines Advisory Committee Report. In addition, a modeling this is certainly recent discovered that a healthy vegetarian diet may have a 42 to 84 percent lower burden on the environment than other dietary patterns. Finally, a report that is new the EAT-Lancet Commission on Food, Planet and Health further supports the link between diet and environment, calling for a international shift to predominately plant-based dietary patterns to improve health and sustainability outcomes.

Plant-based vitamins and diets

Whole food, plant based diets can be the optimal diet to ward off certain cancers, diabetes and obesity versus a 'western diet' that is standard. Nonetheless, vegetarians and especially vegans may need a tad bit more planning when it comes to getting enough of the following minerals and nutrients: iron, calcium, selenium, vitamin D, vitamin B12, and omega–3 omega-6 this is certainly and acids.

•   Vitamin B12 – an supplement that is important the metabolism of every cell in the human anatomy, it is involved in the production of red blood cells and nerve cells. B12 is found only in animal products and is from that is absent foods, unless they've been fortified. Plant based products such as; soy-milk, some breakfast cereals and some meat analogues can be fortified, always check the packaging. The amount of B12 each needs that is person on age and it may be necessary to supplement your diet with an oral B12 supplement, if recommended by your doctor or dietician.

•	Selenium – another mineral that is essential cannot be produced by our figures, selenium plays an important role as part of your immune system and is an antioxidant in low doses. This means it can protect our bodies against free radicals (foreign bodies caused by external sources such as smoking, pollution that can cause our bodies damage). Selenium is usually found in animal based products such meats which are as eggs, and fish. The best sources within plant based are that is foods brazil nuts, sunflower seeds, brown rice and beans. As little as two brazil nuts per day shall provide you with your quota for the day.

- Calcium- is needed for strong bones and teeth but it is also used in many other areas of the human anatomy, for example blood clotting muscle tissue contraction that is and. Meals sources include dairy products, soy, collard greens, broccoli and tofu. Plant based of that is sources may be less bioavailable than dairy based products due to two compounds known as oxalate and phytate found within the plant. These inhibit calcium absorption within body that is the. So ensure you are getting ample calcium through fortified services and products where you can or supplement needed this is certainly if. Especially true for vegan diet plans, or veggie diets which also exclude dairy.

- Iron– plays a role this is certainly vital immune system function, moving oxygen around our bodies through our bloodstream via our haemoglobin and contributing to normal energy levels.

Plant based foods contain a type of iron known as non-heme iron. This of that is type is less easily absorbed (bioavailable) to us compared to the iron discovered in animal based products known as heme-iron. This is due to the fact the non-heme iron must undergo a supplementary chemical conversion within our bodies to make absorbable that is it.

Vitamin C helps or bodies to absorb this type of iron so try to pair plant sources that is based iron with a resource of vitamin C when planning your meals. Plant based sources of iron include: lentils, tofu, chickpeas, beans, chia seeds, ground linseed, hemp seeds, pumpkin seeds, kale, dried apricots, dried figs, raisins and quinoa. Try to pair these with vitamin C containing foods such as broccoli and fruits that is citrus boost the bioavailability of iron. Otherwise, if you are just your that is reducing consumption try to pick animal based products with higher iron levels on the days you do choose to have meat. For example: beef, chicken, canned sardines, or tuna.

Vitamin D– this vitamin is required for the consumption of calcium into our bodies, thus contributing to the development of powerful bones. Our anatomical bodies produce Vitamin D when exposed sunshine this is certainly to. In the UNITED KINGDOM and Ireland during the winter months it is necessary to get Vitamin D from your diet. Foods such as fish that is fatty tuna, mackerel and salmon provide vitamin D. If you are following a plant based diet which excludes fish it will be necessary to supplement with vitamin D. Speak to your doctor, dietician or nutritionist about the best supplement for your needs.

Essential Fatty Acids (Omega-3 and Omega-6)– fat is an macronutrient that is vital is utilized by the body as an energy source and helps the body to absorb particular minerals A, D, E and K.

There two this is certainly are of important fats that we need which the body cannot make it self. These the that is are (alpha-linoleic acid), which is linked to the prevention of diabetes and some cancersand Om ega-6 (linoleic acid) fatty acids.

Resources of omega-6 (LA) include: hemp seeds, sunflower seeds, walnuts and soy spread products. If you are eating a varied range of foods whilst following a based that is plant you will be getting enough of this in your diet.

Omega-3 (ALA) on the other hand is found in high amounts in oily fish such as mackerel, tuna and salmon and may be somewhat harder to obtain on an exclusively vegan or vegetarian based diet. A week in your diet to ensure you are getting adequate ALA if you are just limiting your meat intake, try to include at least one-two portions of oily fish. If you are switching to an exclusively plant based diet be sure to include plant that is plenty of sources of omega-3 per week, such as: chia seeds, canola oil, surface flaxseeds, walnut, soybeans and tofu.

Veggies That Can Substitute for Meat

Tofu, Tempeh, Seitan, and TVP

You may not think of tofu or tempeh veggies which are as but they are plant-based and made from soybeans. TVP, or texturized protein that is vegetable is also made from soy. Seitan is produced from wheat gluten. The in this is certainly meat recipe can be replaced with one of these plant-based options. Tofu makes the perfect swap-out for chicken whether you want Crispy Tofu Nuggets, Moroccan Cutlets inside a Sauce that is lemon-Olive chunks for Chinese food like Kung Pao Tofu. Tempeh is wonderful for fish dishes because it has a texture that is flaky. Try it in "Crab" Cakes or to make breaded fillets that is"Fish. It can also be ground up to act as ground beef for Tempeh Meatballs or tacos. TVP comes in all shapes and sizes and it can replace any meat surface meat that is including. Try it in this Chik'n Salad with Cranberries and Pistachios or in Tacos Sin Carne. Seitan can be flavored to taste exactly like beef or pork. You won't believe the decadence you will get in a dish of Balsamic BBQ Seitan Ribs or a thick, juicy Seitan Steak in Beurre Blanc Sauce.

Mushrooms

When you want that meaty taste, that umami, mushrooms are the way to go. Their flavor is rich, earthy, and meaty, particularly cremini or Portobello mushrooms. They healthy that is are filling and can replace meat in almost any recipe. My favorite way to eat mushrooms is to saute all of them in vegan butter and include thyme, black pepper, and vinegar that is balsamic. Then we serve them over polenta unless I'm piling them up on a crispy roll to make a French Dip sandwich. Try mushrooms in this Mushroom Stroganoff or as a vegan "Lamb" Burger. Impress your guests that are dinner serving them crammed Mushrooms with Pecans and Portobello Wellington .

Jackfruit

If you have not tried that is yet, you need to go out and obtain some. Technically, jackfruit is a fruit but incredibly, it can stand in for beef in savory dishes. You can buy it raw or slice that is already in a will. Jackfruit has a very minor taste that is sweet not so much that you can't use it to make a decadent, satisfying Philly Cheesesteak. Jackfruit is perfect for barbecue sandwiches, stir-fries, or dish that is any uses beef, chicken, or pork.

Eggplant

When anyone goes veg, eggplant is probably the first vegetable that comes to mind, but you can do so much more with it than just make parmigiana. Eggplant has a rich, meaty style and it's very versatile. You will change your mind in the event that you think you're not a fan of eggplant, try it in these Eggplant Burgers and. Other delicious ways to eat include that are eggplant Mozzarella-Stuffed Eggplant Meatballs, crispy Eggplant Fries with Marinara Dipping Sauce, and spiralized Eggplant Noodles.

Lentils

Lentils have always been a for that is stand-in since the beginning of veganism. Lentils are hearty and replace that is can beef easily. Lentils come in a variety of colors such as green, red, brown, and black. They cook up quickly, are inexpensive, and a small amount goes a way this is certainly very long. Definite recipes to try are Red Lentil Burgers with Kale Pesto, Lentil Meatballs, Double Decker Lentil Tacos, and South Indian Lentil Stew.

Beans and Legumes

Beans and legumes amazing that is are. They are inexpensive, healthy, filling, and there so that is are to choose from: black beans, kidney beans, pinto beans, aduki beans, chickpeas and black-eyed peas, to name only a few. Beans make for hearty soups, stews, and chilis. How about a White Bean and Kale Soup or even a Bowl with that is tamale-Inspired beans? Beans and legumes can replace the meat to make Hoisin that is incredible Black Burgers, Black-Eyed Pea Italian Sausages, or Chickpea "Tuna" Salad.

Cauliflower

Right now we bet you're reasoning, "How can cauliflower animal meat that is replace? It's so white and bland." Really, it can. When you season it and cook it up right, cauliflower can be the star of any meal. We like to use cauliflower to replace the chicken in dishes that are asian Cauliflower Manchurian and even Buffalo wings. You can slice the cauliflower into steaks and make an incredible Cauliflower Piccata. You may even make a pizza crust out of cauliflower.

Potatoes

Potatoes are perhaps not just for side dishes. They can be the main ingredient in so dishes that is many. Bake them, mash them, or fry them, potatoes are always a favorite whether you roast all of them, boil them. Begin your meal with a Potato and Cauliflower that is creamy Soup. Potato Samosas with Coconut-Mint Chutney are spicy and tasty. Add potatoes your that is to like in this Moussaka Burger with Béchamel Cheese Sauce and also this Spicy Potato Cauliflower Burger. Don't forget potatoes when it comes to that's dessert right. You will be away that is blown this Chocolate Potato Cake.

Beets

Beets are candy that is nature's. They are sweet and delicious and perfect for salads, but they have actually another to them that is side. Beets also that is are and work well in savory dishes especially when roasted as in this Sesame Roasted Beets and Greens Dish. Amaze your guests with a platter that is beautiful of Carpaccio and then treat them to Roasted Beet Burgers with Cumin-

Scented Ketchup. Finish the meal with Beetroot Chocolate Frosted Cupcakes.

Peanuts

 Ok, technically, nuts are not vegetables but they can be used to make vegan cheese and to exchange meat in your cooking. Nuts can be" that is incredibly"meaty can make a hearty and rich "meat" loaf for dinner. Nuts are often added to vegan burgers for added "meatiness." Try these Kidney Bean –Walnut Burgers with Mississippi Comeback Sauce.

As you can see, when it comes meat that is to replacing your meals, your options are practically limitless. Stop thinking vegetables which are of side dishes and move them to the front of your dish. With all the hearty, "meaty" recipes you can create, there is way that is no will miss the meat.

Those after a diet this is certainly plant-based need certainly to plan their meals a little more carefully. Arming yourself with some dietary information can make most of the difference. You might find it to that is useful our guides on vegetarian sources of protein, where you can obtain vitamin B12 as well as the best plant resources of omega-3.

Weekly if you are significantly changing your diet, it may be useful to start slowly – perhaps presenting two or three plant-based meals, or days. This your that is allows to adapt to new foods and to the changes in the proportion of certain nutrients, such as fibre. It also allows you to experiment with brand-new meals and build up some storecupboard staples over a period time this is certainly of.